Mental Health:
A Christian
Approach

About the Authors
and Respondent

MARK P. COSGROVE

Mark Cosgrove is an assistant professor of psychology at Taylor University, in Upland, Indiana. He obtained his B.A. at Creighton University, and his M.S. and Ph.D. in experimental psychology from Purdue University. He was a visiting assistant professor in the Department of Psychology at Purdue in the fall of 1973 before serving as a research associate with Probe Ministries International from 1974 to 1976. He is a member of Sigma Xi, the Midwestern Psychological Association, and the American Scientific Affiliation. Dr. Cosgrove has published frequently in *Vision Research* and in *Perception and Psychophysics*.

JAMES D. MALLORY, JR.

James Mallory is the Director of the Atlanta Counseling Center. He is a graduate of Princeton University and received his M.D. from Duke University Medical School, where he did his internship in internal medicine, and his residency in psychiatry. He remained in the Department of Psychiatry at Duke as a clinical instructor and later as an assistant professor of psychiatry. Before his present position at Atlanta Counseling Center, he served as its medical director. Dr. Mallory is the author of *The Kink and I*.

O. QUENTIN HYDER

Quentin Hyder maintains a private psychiatry practice in New York City and is medical director of the Christian Counseling and Psychotherapy Center in midtown Manhattan. He is also involved in clinical research at the Columbia-Presbyterian Medical Center. He received his M.D. from Cambridge University and the London Hospital and obtained his psychiatric training at Columbia University. He is a member of the American Psychiatric Association, the Christian Medical Society, and the Christian Association for Psychological Studies.

Mental Health: A Christian Approach

Mark P. Cosgrove
and
James D. Mallory, Jr.

with a response by
O. Quentin Hyder

ZONDERVAN PUBLISHING HOUSE
OF THE ZONDERVAN CORPORATION
GRAND RAPIDS, MICHIGAN 49506

PROBE MINISTRIES
INTERNATIONAL
RICHARDSON, TEXAS 75080

Copyright   © 1977 by Probe Ministries International

Library of   Cosgrove, Mark P
Congress   Mental health: a Christian approach.
Cataloging in
Publication Data   (Christian free university curriculum)
Bibliography: p.
1. Psychology, Pathological.   2. Mental health.
3. Psychotherapy.   4. Christianity—Psychology,
I. Mallory, James D., joint author.   II. Title.
III. Series.
RC454.C658   616.8'9   77-2694

ISBN   0-310-35721-7

Place of
Printing   *Printed in the United States of America*

Permissions

page 12   Courtesy of H. Armstrong Roberts. Statistics from *Abnormal Psychology* by James C. Coleman. 4th ed. Glenview,
Ill.: Scott, Foresman & Co., 1972.

page 23   From Brady, J. V., Porter, R.W., Conrad, D.G., and Mason, J.W., "Avoidance behavior and the development of
gastroduodenal ulcers." Courtesy of *Journal of the Experimental Analysis of Behavior,* 1958 , *1,* 69–72 (photo on p.
70). Copyright 1958 by the Society for the Experimental
Analysis of Behavior, Inc.

page 24   Courtesy of Paul Lewis

page 57   From Lars Leksell, *Stereotoxic and Radio Surgery,* 1971.
Courtesy of Charles C. Thomas, Publisher, Springfield, Ill.

Design   Cover design by Paul Lewis
Book design by Louise Bauer

What is Probe?

Probe Ministries is a nonprofit corporation organized to provide perspective on the integration of the academic disciplines and historic Christianity. The members and associates of the Probe team are actively engaged in research as well as lecturing and interacting in thousands of university classrooms throughout the United States and Canada on topics and issues vital to the university student.

Christian Free University books should be ordered from Zondervan Publishing House, but further information about Probe's materials and ministries may be obtained by writing to Probe Ministries International, Box 5012, Richardson, Texas 75080.

Book Abstract

The central elements of a Christian approach to mental health and psychotherapy are examined. These elements include an examination of the nature of man, the sources of mental problems, and the goals for mental health. With this as a basis, five distinctive elements that Christian psychotherapy contributes to the actual counseling process are discussed.

Contents

Illustrations

A Viable
Viewpoint

Chapter Abstract

Comparisons are made between historical and modern approaches to mental problems. Growing Christian approaches to counseling are explained and general questions are examined.

A Viable Viewpoint

While earlier centuries were labeled the "Age of Enlightenment" or the "Age of Reason," many have labeled our own century the "Age of Anxiety." Such is the magnitude of emotional problems in our society.

One authority estimates that forty million persons in the United States suffer from some type of mental problem.[1] These millions are individuals who suffer continuous emotional discomfort, behave in bizarre ways, or are unable to perform their major life roles adequately. They include approximately ten million neurotics, nine million alcoholics, six million mentally retarded, five million emotionally disturbed children, four million antisocial personalities, two million psychotics, and one million hard-drug addicts. In addition to these more serious disturbances in mental health, millions of other Americans occasionally lose any enjoyment in living through excessive grief, anxiety, worry, and depression. From these facts it should be clear that mental problems represent the biggest 11

Mental Health:
A Christian
Perspective

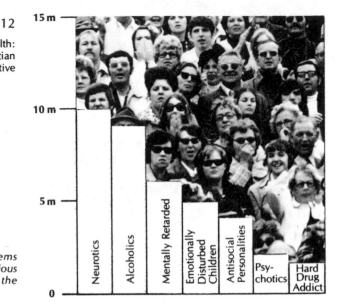

15 m

10 m

5 m

Neurotics

Alcoholics

Mentally Retarded

Emotionally Disturbed Children

Antisocial Personalities

Psy-chotics

Hard Drug Addict

0

Mental problems have reached serious proportions in the United States.

health issues in our society and that no one is immune.

A survey of past approaches to mental problems reveals some astute diagnoses and helpful care, as well as an abundance of ignorance, superstition, and fear. Hippocrates (460-360 B.C.), the father of modern medicine, and Avicenna (A.D. 980-1037), an outstanding figure in Arabic medicine, made many accurate observations with regard to the natural causes of mental illness. However, early Chinese, Egyptian, and Greek cultures, as well as the European culture of the Middle Ages, considered the spirit world to be the primary cause of bizarre behaviors and convulsive attacks. Treatments, accordingly, ranged from kindly rest homes to incantations, physical abuse, and imprisonment.

As we approach our own time, we have seen the rise of more moral and more scientific approaches to mental problems. Modern approaches are more moral because of today's belief that many of the mentally disturbed are essentially normal individuals who could profit from a more favorable environment and some professional help with personal problems, and who are

worth the efforts these require. Modern approaches are
more scientific because research efforts have provided
the basis for better diagnostic methods and a variety of
medical and psychological therapies.

In general, current psychotherapies have emerged
from schools of thought that have constructed varying
models of man and his problems. The major approaches to psychotherapy include medical,
psychoanalytic, behavioristic, humanistic, existential,
and interpersonal methods. Christian counseling and
psychotherapy also must be included as a major approach to solving mental problems. The influence of
Christian approaches to counseling is becoming increasingly widespread because more and more individuals with a strong Christian commitment are entering the counseling profession. Even though these
Christian psychotherapists may select from a variety of
methods of the differing psychological schools of
thought, they are unified by a common model of man
and his problems. As with the other schools of thought,
there may be some variations within the model.
Nevertheless, this model stems from biblical information about man and has a significant impact on
the counseling process.

The importance of Christian counseling, though,
has often been ignored or misunderstood, generally,
because of the antiscience bias, or the "witchhunts,"
of the church of the Middle Ages. While these past em-
phases by the church are not to be denied or defended,
we must realize that this is hardly the picture of Christian approaches to mental health today. Some readers
may feel such biases remain in all things Christian, and
the authors are sympathetic toward this concern. However, the reader is encouraged to defer final conclu-
sions and take up the role of an investigator. The
scientific method and its data are available to the Christian psychotherapist, and he seeks to integrate this data
with information from the Bible, which he believes is
God's description of man and his problems (Meehl, et
al., 1958; Peters, 1969; Ellison, 1972; Farnsworth,
1975; Greer, 1975; Jackson, 1975; Sall, 1975).[2] The
assumptions of such an integrative process between

Christianity and psychology are summarized by Carter and Mohline (1976):

(a) All truth is God's truth, therefore, the truths of psychology (general revelation) are neither contradictory nor contrary to revealed truth (special revelation) but are integrative in a harmonious whole. (b) Theology represents the distillation of God's revelation of Himself to man in a linguistic, conceptual, and cultural media man can understand and which focuses primarily on man's nature and destiny in God's program. (c) Psychology as a science is primarily concerned with the mechanisms by which man functions and the methods to assess that functioning. Nevertheless, the content of psychology as a science (including theory) provides a statement on the nature and functioning of man.[3]

The usefulness of such an integrative process between the data of psychology and biblical teaching on man can be appreciated if we recognize that the scientific method has limitations in giving us a complete, "whole" view of man. The scientific method can encompass only that which is observable and readily measurable. Biblical revelation, on the other hand, gives an overarching view of man and his condition. (See *The Essence of Human Nature*, 1977.) This viewpoint is consistent with scientific understanding, and from it the data of psychology can be discussed and interpreted.

Contradictions between psychological theory and statements in the Bible do arise, but such contradictions are insufficient in themselves to dismiss the biblical view of man as inaccurate, just as one scientific theory is not thrown out because it conflicts with another scientific theory. In fact, scientific theories are frequently in conflict with one another. They are not beyond error, since science presents a very fluid picture of man, and this scientific picture is constantly changing as the data collection progresses. A scientist should not treat his models of man as if they are final and exhaustive truth. Such models are merely ways to encompass the data that has been collected thus far.

In addition, one should realize that most conflicts between psychology and Christianity are *not over the data* of psychology, but *over the interpretation* of the data. For example, the Christian psychologist ap-

preciates that man's behavior is modified by positive
and negative reinforcements, but he resists the fatalistic determinism of some behaviorists or psycho-
analysts. He finds that his biblical view of the voli-
tional aspect of man is more compatible with the
humanistic psychologist's interpretation of the same
behavioral data. Therefore, the Christian psychologist
is not in disagreement with science, but only with
specific interpretations of scientific data.

Many contradictions between psychology and theology are only apparent and would not arise if in each
field there existed a better understanding of the language used in the other. Viktor Frankl (developer of
logotherapy) and Billy Graham do not have the same
meaning when they speak of man's spiritual nature.
Another example is the use of the word *conversion*.
The psychological term usually means a pathological
state in which the person is dealing with unconscious
conflicts by suddenly developing clinical symptoms.
The Christian term means that a man's relationship
with God has been restored by a faith commitment to
Jesus Christ; it is sometimes referred to as being "born
again." To misunderstand such terms can lead psychologists or theologians to disagree on a topic, when
in fact they are using the same words but not referring
to the same phenomena in man's being or experience.

We, the authors, assume that an effective psychotherapy can proceed from an integration of the scientific and the biblical views of man and his problems.
In this study we will examine, in general, the central
elements of a Christian view of mental health common
to most types of Christian psychotherapy. We will
begin with an examination of the nature of man,
sources of his problems, and the goals for mental
health. With this basis we will then discuss the distinctive qualities of a Christian approach to psychotherapy.

A Description
of Human Nature

Chapter Abstract

Different practices of psychotherapy often depend on different definitions of the nature of man. Various definitions, with their one-, two-, or three-dimensional views of man, are explained.

A Description of Human Nature

A brief description of the nature of man is important to any view of mental health, because such a view provides the boundaries within which the psychotherapist is willing to discuss the sources of man's mental problems and the appropriate solutions. Quite often it is an emphasis on a special aspect of human nature that has led psychotherapists to practice a particular type of psychotherapy. For example, psychoanalytic, behavioristic, and humanistic counselors have different views of man's inherent make-up, and consequently they arrive at different explanations as to the sources of his problems. The *psychoanalytic* school of psychotherapy feels that abnormal behavior stems from unconscious conflicts within the inner personality and the attempts to relieve those conflicts. The *behavioristic* school sees abnormal behavior as originating from a response to environmental pressures. The *humanistic* school of psychology emphasizes the conscious person's struggle to develop 19 into a fully actualized human being. Since these schools of psychology see different sources of man's problems, each offers a different therapy for the same symptoms of an emotionally troubled person.

Likewise, any distinctively Christian approach to treating the emotionally disturbed must have its basis in a Christian view of man's nature. A distinguishing mark of a Christian view of man is that it avoids an overemphasis on any single aspect of man's being, but considers his entire nature. For this reason, Christian psychotherapists consider, as a factor in proper mental health, the spiritual needs of man defined by Jesus Christ in the Bible. In general, the Christian view of man speaks of several aspects or dimensions to one's whole, unified being. Different aspects of man's nature seem appropriate for interacting with and appreciating physical, mental, and spiritual dimensions of reality. Let us look at each of these three in turn.

Human Nature is Physical

It is more than obvious that man has a body and bodily needs and must relate successfully to physical aspects of his environment. We all need food, oxygen, and sleep and we need to be able to make a proper physical response to stress in our environment. Some psychologists have concluded that physical needs must be met before the higher needs of man can be dealt with effectively. Abraham Maslow argued that human motives can be arranged into a hierarchy. He felt that when the biological needs of an individual are satisfied, then that person is free to seek the satisfaction of higher needs, such as safety, love, and esteem.[4]

The tendency exists, though, to describe human nature as if it is limited to the realm of the physical. B. F. Skinner's behavioristic theories, evolutionary theory, and books like *The Naked Ape*[5] have popularized such a one-dimensional view of mankind. These views go to great lengths to explain away mankind's complex behaviors that stem from his non-physical needs. Freud, for example, felt that complex human behaviors, including religious worship, were only displaced motives, i.e., those in which physical

energy has been channeled into more socially acceptable areas. Likewise, B. F. Skinner, without recourse
to nonphysical concepts like the "self" or the
"mind," explains complex human behavior by the
concept of secondary reinforcement. Thus, he would
explain the creative activity of the poet to be stimulated
by money, a secondary reinforcer, with its power to
compel derived from the primary reinforcer, the food it
will buy. In secondary reinforcement, nonphysical
stimuli become reinforcers and motivators of human
behavior because of their close association with physical or primary rewards.

The results of such limited views of man become
apparent in psychotherapy. Because strict behaviorists
do not believe in the mind, they cannot believe in
mental problems, only problems in behavior. Such
views are seriously limited in their capacity to remedy
human ills. Most therapists, on the other hand, consider abnormal behavior as symptomatic of deeper
mental problems. There can be no denying that the
physical dimension of man has a great bearing on
mental health. However, denying the self-conscious,
free, human mind, and all the higher aspirations and
needs of man limits the scope of human problems that
strict behaviorists can treat.

**Human Nature
is Mental**

It may sound as if we are stating the obvious to say
that man has a mind, but the influence of behaviorism
is so strong today that it is requiring a major revolution
in the form of humanistic psychology to give a more
complete view of man. Man's mental dimension involves tangible qualities of self that are interrelated
with the physical brain and environmental stimuli.
However, man's mind goes beyond the physical and
gives him the capacity to enter into special human
relationships and to engage in self-conscious thought.[6]
Because he has these capacities (and hence needs) to
relate to himself and to others, he is vulnerable to
problems in these areas when these "human" needs
are blocked.

Humanistic psychologists such as Abraham Maslow
and Carl Rogers rightly assert that human beings have

goals, need people, and are active and free with respect to their environments.[7] Consequently, their approaches to psychotherapy emphasize the *humanness* of man and not his *animalness*. A similar emphasis is seen in the work of Harry Stack Sullivan, Erich Fromm, Karen Horney, and Eric Berne, who have described man as a social being with interpersonal needs.[8] Repeatedly, the idea is stressed that people are not things. They need to be properly related to themselves and to others, lest emotional problems arise.

Many psychologists and psychiatrists use this two-dimensional (physical and mental) approach in dealing with human emotional problems. Some believe man's two dimensions are open to each other and that emotional problems are psychosomatic, i.e., involved with the interaction of man's mind *(psyche)* and his body *(soma)*. In other words, physical problems will affect your mind and mental stress can produce physical ailments.[9]

The classic experiment of "ulcers in executive monkeys" demonstrates this fact.[10] In this experiment two monkeys were given electrical shocks every twenty seconds, while they were restrained in their chairs. One of the monkeys could avoid the shock for both by pressing a lever at least once every twenty seconds. Both animals received the shocks; but the one who assumed an element of responsibility over the situation developed ulcers as a result of the continued stress, while the other did not.

Psychosomatic problems are common for human beings because our thinking, desiring, remembering, and imagining can produce physiological tensions at high levels over extended periods of time. The well-publicized studies of Type A (anxious) and Type B (not anxious) individuals have shown that an anxious person has a greater vulnerability to heart disease.[11] Because of the impact of emotional stress on the physical, the counselor must take into account what physiological damage a person has sustained during his emotional stress and how this and other biological changes in his system are now affecting his mind's ability to respond to continued stress or frustration.

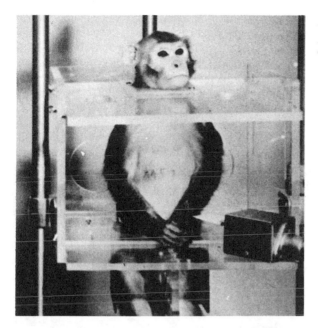

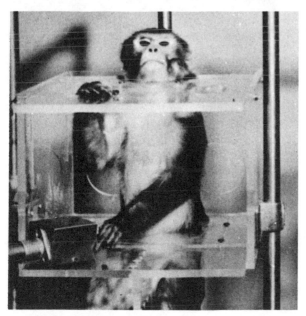

The "executive monkey" (bottom) avoids the electrical shocks for both monkeys by pressing a lever. By assuming some responsibility, this monkey develops ulcers because of the stress, while the other monkey (top) does not.

**Human Nature
is Spiritual**

There is emerging in psychology a growing awareness that man seems equipped to relate, not only to his world, himself, and other persons, but also to "other-worldly," or spiritual, reality. Some animals have well-developed minds and apparent use of free will, but the human being transcends these qualities and appears to be overequipped for just this world.

We can observe this truth in three ways. First, we find man everywhere on his knees worshiping,

Humans everywhere demonstrate spiritual capacities and awarenesses. They appear to be "incurable worshipers."

strongly aware, somehow, that there is a being higher than himself. He has the idea of an Ideal. Second, he carries within himself standards that are higher than he apparently can meet. These standards may vary from culture to culture, but every man and culture has a highly developed moral sense. Third, man evidently is not satisfied by the things of this world, psychological or physical. Animals can eat, drink, and have sex; and life apparently is complete for them. Men can satisfy their physical needs, then gain fame, family, friends, money, power, and excitement, and not be through.

Still they experience frustration, emptiness, and lack of fulfillment; the quest seems endless.

To reduce these three evidences of man's spiritual nature to solely mental aspects is to ignore the context in which they are always found, i.e., the context of a Supreme Being and man's attempts to find Him. Man deals with a spiritual dimension, and, either consciously or unconsciously, acts as if it is real, and as if he needs to be a part of it. In order to deal with mental health on a purely biological or mental level, a psychotherapist must ignore the reality of these spiritual concerns. However, when the psychotherapist and the client become involved in the problems of existence and the meaning of life, of moral values and guilt, then effective counseling can take place only with a frame of reference that recognizes the value of religious beliefs and moral behavior. This spiritual awareness and capacity of man has an enormous impact on his mind, and therefore man's proper relationship to God and morality are of central concern for Christian counselors.

Some individuals decry any treatment of man that views him as spiritual or beyond scientific description. They maintain that he is reducible to scientific explanation alone. However, it must be remembered that reducing man to his most easily measured aspect, his body, however scientifically rigorous, is far from adequate in developing a comprehensive mental health model. Although science is rightfully a servant to reality, it is possible to place reality in unnatural subjection to science and its confining limitations.

A Christian counselor, who goes beyond the physical and the mental in his approach to man, is doing no more than what is already being done in many areas of psychology. Viktor Frankl openly discusses the spiritual dimension of man, which he describes in terms of freedom, responsibility, will-to-meaning, and some elements of transcendence.[12] Transpersonal psychologists, who are studying the effects of hallucinogenic drugs, meditative techniques, and ESP, are seeking ways to help man transcend his person to higher, spiritual levels.

A Christian counselor can develop his counseling approach based on a description of man's mental, physical, and spiritual nature, and still ground his methods in science, as will be seen in this study, and proceed with a view to testing the effectiveness of his chosen methods.

**Human Nature
Is Fallen**

The idea that an inherent character flaw is common to all men also has a bearing on our discussion of mental health. The question of whether man is good or evil has often been dealt with but never satisfactorily answered by any school of psychology. Freud pointed out the evil lurking within us: our aggressive, sexual, and death instincts, which are unconscious and irrational. But proponents of this view have difficulty explaining all the goodness and nobility we do find in man. The humanistic psychologist says that man may have some bad qualities, but, for the most part, it is his nature to do good; and, if left alone, he will drift in that direction. Maslow said, speaking of man's nature:

> Since this inner nature is good or neutral rather than bad, it is best to bring it out, to encourage it rather than to suppress it. If it is permitted to guide our life, we grow healthy, fruitful, and happy.[13]

The trouble with the humanistic outlook, though, is the historical record of six thousand years of human cruelty, war, greed, crime, and mental conflict that we must overlook. The behaviorist enters the debate and seeks to explain both good and evil in human behavior by saying that man is neutral. He will become good or bad, depending on the nature of his environment. John Watson, the father of American behaviorism, put it simply in this now-famous sentence:

> Give me a dozen healthy infants, well-formed, and my own specific world to bring them up in and I'll guarantee to take anyone at random and train him to become any type of specialist I might select — doctor, lawyer, artist, merchant-chief, and yes even beggarman and thief.[14]

The problem with this position, both historically and presently, is that man's problems have defied environmental boundaries. He commits crimes, gets divorces, etc., in all segments of society; that is, from both good and bad environments.

The Christian view of man (amplified later) recognizes tendencies to both good and evil present within man. Succinctly, the Christian view explains that man aspires to good because he is created in God's image, but it is impossible for man not to "sin" because he is born alienated from God, and thus is self-

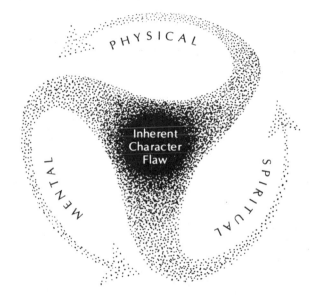

Although man at times aspires to good, it is impossible for him to constantly reach this goal because of an inherent character flaw.

centered at birth. Consequently, life is a struggle to become other-centered. This Christian view of man offers an explanation for much that is paradoxical about man's nature. For example, to the humanistic psychologist, who emphasizes man's natural goodness, it is perplexing why so few, if any, human beings ever become truly good. Maslow's hierarchy of human motives stressed that humans are approaching a state of being self-actualized, healthy and fully functioning; and yet he remarks:

There are certainly good and strong and successful men in the world. . . . But it also remains true that there are so few of them, even though there could be so many more.[15]

This same unfulfilled condition of man is found by those who study human moral development. Lawrence Kohlberg speaks of stages of morality through which all individuals pass, gradually progressing toward a more other-centered morality.[16] Unfortunately, most adults never get beyond a morality that is motivated by a desire for approval or by some external authority. Usually, man's generosity toward and concern for others is motivated by a desire to gain personal rewards through secondary means. It is as if man does not have the inherent power to realize his potential goodness sufficiently.

The transpersonal psychologist, observing man's limitations in using his potential, believes that man is cut off from higher realities and that he must transcend his present being to a higher conscious reality via meditation, drugs, or religious mysticism. The ultimate purpose of these techniques is to help man find the inner peace and rest that is so notably absent in human nature. The Christian agrees that man is cut off from the higher reality of God, but he says there is nothing man can do by himself to restore his lost potential and peace; that is a task for God, who invites men into a personal relationship with Himself through Jesus Christ.

The learning theory of the behaviorist also describes aspects of the "fallen" nature of man. Strict behaviorists see man as a machine without freedom (Skinner, 1971).[17] Ruch and Zimbardo devote a chapter to forces that diminish man. In it they described this best when they labeled a section "Surrender of Responsibility: The Paradox of Freedom."[18] Man has freedom, but much of the time he is victimized by his environment and the rewards it holds for him. In the Christian view, the reason for this paradox is that man's world revolves around himself and, therefore, self-control becomes extremely difficult. It is easy to be selfish and difficult to be concerned for others. Very soon, in many areas of our lives, the environment does become the controller as we surrender our freedoms for our wants.

A good example of this flaw in the human character is the tendency of most individuals to obey authority even when it is an immoral one, just as did many citizens of Nazi Germany during World War II. The classic experiments of Stanley Milgram showed that individuals would deliver what seemed to be agonizingly painful electrical shocks to a confederate subject, because of a prior agreement to submit to the authority of the experimenter.[19] The experiment, supposedly, was to determine the effects of punishment on memory. The shock administrators, ordered to administer increasingly powerful shocks, became apprehensive that their confederate subjects were suffering much greater pain than the administrators had assumed they would. Yet, 62 percent of the administrators continued to increase the amount of shock to a full dosage, sometimes to the point that the subjects seemed to pass out. None of the administrators, who represented a wide cross-section of the population, wanted to punish their victims or appeared to get sadistic thrills out of their tasks; many even protested. The real subjects, of course, were these administrators, whose willingness to obey or disobey the authority of the experimenter was being tested. The confederate subjects never received any shocks and their agony was only an act.

The Christian view again explains this problem. Man, because of his sin nature, can reach the depths of evil. It is culture and learning that restrain most people. Take away the restraints of society in a local emergency such as a flood, or add a crowd for everyone to hide in, and common John Doe throws rocks through windows and loots the stores. The point is that our "good" behavior is often a result of strong social or civil restraints, which may conceal the potential for bad behavior present in everyone.

This lengthy discussion of the fallen nature of humanity is intended to show some of the pressures put on people as they strive for fulfillment and happiness. There are counter pressures within them that work against mental health. These pressures, which stem from humanity's alienation from God, lead to alienation from others, an overconcern for self, lack of meaning and purpose, a deterioration of self-image, and a lack of power to improve sufficiently to resist the pull of the environment.

Sources of
Emotional Problems

Chapter Abstract

Various definitions of normal and abnormal behavior are considered as well as possible sources of harmful behavior. Sources discussed are heredity, biological factors, beliefs, actions, reactions, and unmet spiritual needs.

chapter three

Sources of Emotional Problems

In discussing the difficult question of the causes of emotional problems, we wish to emphasize that mental problems stem from a variety of sources, because man is a complex, multidimensional being. We see predisposing factors (factors that make individuals vulnerable to mental problems) at every level of his being — physical, mental, and spiritual. The interaction of these factors over time produces the twisted lives that we find in the counseling office. We wish to introduce this section with a brief discussion of what is normal and abnormal behavior, and briefly examine the types of emotional disturbance.

Before discussing abnormal behavior and its causes, we need to define the concept of abnormality. One of the definitions of abnormality is a statistical measure. If we measure a large group of individuals for a certain characteristic, we will find that most individuals fall

Normal Versus Abnormal Behavior

33

within a median range on that characteristic. That statistical range we will call "normal." If anyone is outside of that range, he would be labeled "abnormal," which literally means "away from the normal" (*ab*-normal). Generally, this is a cultural definition, with individuals being compared to other individuals within their culture.

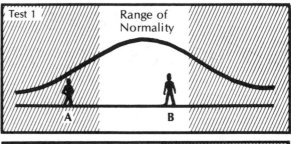

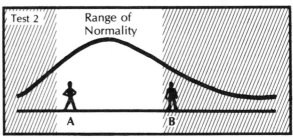

The statistical range for abnormality is dependent on the numbers of people experiencing a particular problem; so a person considered normal on one scale could be abnormal on another.

RANGE OF BEHAVIOR

The problem with this definition of abnormality is that the concept of who is emotionally disturbed changes with the numbers of people experiencing a particular problem. In 1974 the American Psychiatric Association scratched homosexuality from its list of personality disorders. The large numbers of homosexuals in this country was part of the reason for this action. One day a homosexual is disturbed. The next day he is not. What if a whole society shows extreme alienation or hostility? Shall we call it normal and healthy? Dr. Donald Campbell, while president of the American Psychological Association, accused psychologists of this practice of adjusting norms when he said:

All the dominant modern psychologies are in-
dividualistically hedonistic, explaining all human behavior in terms of individual pleasure and pain, individual
needs and drives. They not only describe man as selfishly
motivated, but implicitly or explicitly teach that he ought
to be so.[20]

Obviously, we can look to the norm for a rough idea of
what is abnormal, but this does not provide us with a
useful definition in all cases.

Another definition of abnormal behavior is any behavior that is maladaptive or harmful to the individual
or to society at large. This is a good practical definition
in most cases, but our definition of what is harmful to a
person can vary from counselor to counselor. One
counselor might consider it normal for a man to want to
commit adultery and advise him to do so. By his
definition that may be normal behavior. Certainly, not
every psychotherapist agrees with that as a definition
of normal sexual activity.

It is good to remember that the following terms of
mental illness have come to us from the medical model
of mental illness, which saw abnormal behavior as a
disease with characteristic symptoms. Most psychotherapists admit that not all mental illness is biological in origin and not all abnormal persons should be
considered "ill," as if it is something you catch from a
germ. We will use the terms from the medical model,
however, since they are common and provide an expe-
dient method of roughly classifying symptoms of abnormal behavior. There are many categories of emotional disturbances, but we will define only six that are
of most concern to this monograph. Definitions for
these categories were adapted from the *Diagnostic and
Statistical Manual of Mental Disorders* (2nd ed.) of the
American Psychiatric Association.[21]

**Types of
Abnormality**

1. *Organic brain syndromes*. These are disorders
   caused by or associated with impairment of
   brain tissue function.

2. *Psychoses*. Individuals are described as psychotic when their mental functioning is
   sufficiently impaired to interfere grossly with

their capacity to meet the ordinary demands of life. The impairment may result from a serious distortion in their capacity to recognize reality. Hallucinations and delusions, for example, may distort their perceptions. Alterations in mood may be so profound that the patient's capacity to respond appropriately is grossly impaired. Deficits in perception, language, and memory may be so severe that the patient's capacity for mental grasp of his situation is effectively lost.

3. *Neuroses.* Anxiety is the chief characteristic of neuroses. It may be felt and expressed directly, or it may be controlled unconsciously and automatically by various psychological mechanisms. The neuroses, as contrasted with the psychoses, generally manifest neither gross distortion or misinterpretation of external reality nor gross personality disorganization.

4. *Personality disorders.* This group of disorders is characterized by deeply ingrained maladaptive patterns of behavior that are perceptibly different in quality from psychotic and neurotic symptoms. Generally they are lifelong patterns, often recognizable by the time of adolescence or earlier. They include sexual deviations, alcoholism, and drug dependence.

5. *Psychophysiologic (psychosomatic) disorders.* These disorders are characterized by physical symptoms that are caused by emotional factors and involve a single organ system, for example, the skin or the gastrointestinal system.

6. *Conditions without manifest psychiatric disorder.* This category includes problems of individuals who are psychiatrically normal but who nevertheless have severe problems in marital, social, or occupational adjustment.

Heredity Factors Affect Mental Health

There is strong evidence that hereditary factors can be responsible for tendencies toward some psychoses, such as schizophrenia and manic-depressive illness. It is known that schizophrenia is more common among the close relatives of a schizophrenic than among others, even when those relatives are reared in different environments.[22] Although the evidence favors a hereditary factor in the origin of schizophrenia, we do not know how this susceptibility is transmitted. It is clear that environmental factors play a significant role as well. It can be safely said that most psychotherapists agree that only a predisposition to mental disorder can be inherited.[23]

There is a great deal of evidence for physiological disruptions leading to emotional disturbances. Head injuries, brain tumors, and poisoning by such substances as lead and carbon monoxide have an effect on mental stability. An infection such as syphilis is known to cause general paresis, a disorder characterized by a progressive deterioration of behavior and mental ability. Drug reactions, like those caused by LSD, also give indirect evidence that chemical factors play a part in mental disorders, since an LSD trip can produce symptoms similar to those of psychosis.

**Biological
Factors Affect
Mental Health**

Other biological factors include *cerebral arteriosclerosis* (hardening of the arteries) and the loss of brain cells through aging. Patients in their seventies account for as much as 30 percent of all those admitted to mental hospitals each year. These patients display psychotic disruption of their lives. While brain damage, per se, can produce psychoses in these people in many instances, mild infections, situational problems, or sudden changes in their lives may tip the balance of rational adjustment.

There is also interest in the role of biochemical factors in mental disorders. Abnormalities in brain chemistry apparently lead to the severe emotional disruption and mood swings of the manic-depressive and evidently are connected with many symptoms of schizophrenia. Of course, this is a chicken-or-the-egg question. Which came first? Did the brain chemistry produce the depression or did repeated periods of depression change brain chemistry? We know, for example, that there are psychological factors in the life of the manic-depressive that may precede the chemical change in the nervous system. It is known that a disproportionate number of manic-depressives tend to come from upper socioeconomic groups (a factor that may be inherited but is not genetic!). However, even if psychological factors precede the chemical change in the brain, the fact remains that when treated with drugs, the depression goes away and sometimes does not return.

**Beliefs Affect
Mental Health**

All of us make basic assumptions about ourselves, the character of the world we live in, and God. All of these assumptions contribute to a person's world view, which is a set of conscious and unconscious beliefs attempting to answer the basic questions in life. We strive to answer questions on the meaning of life, life after death, purpose in suffering, and the determining of moral behavior. Much of the emotional stress that we face stems from our having a world view that is not adequate to get us through life, or one that is at odds with the way the world really is.

The existential school of psychology speaks of man's anxiety as coming from his encounter with some unanswerable problem like death. This one, final, human encounter directly challenges every person to develop a world view for his own emotional defense. Unfortunately, many world views are not grounded in authority or well thought out, and leave a person inadequately prepared for life.[24] There are several areas of emotional problems that can grow from inadequate belief systems, such as guilt, a poor self-image, excessive grief, and depression. Christian approaches to psychotherapy are especially equipped to deal with these problems because of their coherent world view, especially where they speak of man and his problems.

**Actions Affect
Mental Health**

When a person behaves in a way counter to his own beliefs or society's expectations, there will be tension in his life. A group of therapies, which we will examine later, have recently attacked some tenets of the medical model of emotional "illness" and have stressed that individuals who exhibit psychopathology are avoiding responsibility for their actions. In other words, there are consequences to human behavior, and some of the consequences, like guilt and shattered interpersonal relationships, affect mental health. This whole issue gets one very quickly into beliefs about morals and sin and determining what is wrong, to whom am I accountable, and how I decide to resolve guilt feelings. All of these have a bearing on emotional adjustment.

"The source of personality problems is a lack of adjustment of tensions within the personality," says Rollo May.[25] If he is correct, and many agree with his statement, then what are the causes of internal mental tensions? In large part, inner tension is due to an individual's failure to adjust properly to environmental pressures and stress, both past and present. Such stress can come from childhood trauma, interpersonal conflict, disease and physical deformity, sexual frustration, failure in areas of life, etc. When an individual is faced with a conflict of motives or a frustrating experience, he can *act* in a direct, reality-oriented way that seeks to remove the problem, or he can *react* by means of defense mechanisms that often involve a flight from reality. For example, an individual may *repress* painful, anxiety-producing memories by pushing them from his consciousness, or rationalize away his failures by finding logical, but false, reasons for his behavior. Another form of reaction is *compartmentalization,* in which a person has a whole body of information, such as deep-seated ethical convictions, so walled off in his head that it has no influence on his day-to-day behavior.

**Reactions Affect
Mental Health**

The Christian's world view declares the reality of God and the spiritual world, man's creation for participation in both physical and spiritual realities, and the historic fall of man that blocks his total participation in spiritual reality. Therefore, every individual is seen as having areas of spiritual need in his life which, if unmet or filled by erroneous substitutes, can affect his mental health.

**Spiritual
Factors Affect
Mental Health**

Modern man particularly needs a sense of hope, protection, guidance, and meaning in a universe that is too often portrayed as mechanistic, chance, cold, and impersonal. Man also needs an answer to death. Death overlooks no one and its ever-present shadow on our world forces each person to think beyond this world to the next.

Many individuals seek to fill spiritual voids such as a lack of meaning in life or the reality of death by a constant search for physical pleasure and comfort. This search for the "good life" produces no lasting peace and meaning. A similar path can be followed by an individual who seeks answers in religion, but who has a distorted view of God. He may see God as harsh and punitive, or Christianity as a list of do's and don'ts. The resulting fear of hell and concern for rules and appearances is enough to rob many individuals of mental peace and joy.

Such individuals need to take part in spiritual realities by entering into an ongoing relationship with a loving God. It is apparent in the Bible that God wants people to live with a certain mind-set in order to know full mental and spiritual health. They must learn to live life with a claim on and a sense of God's forgiveness, even in the face of continued faults and failures. They must live with the confidence that God has a plan for their happiness and well-being in this life and that He provides a source of power to meet every challenge. Furthermore, they must retain the confidence that even when they fail to appropriate that power, God still maintains control. They must believe that God intends to meet their needs now through the body of Christian believers on earth and that they will live after death in eternal joy with Him.

Finally, the Christian also recognizes that the reality of the spiritual world includes the reality of Satan and, consequently, temptations and attacks in vulnerable areas of his emotional and mental make-up.

Goals for Human
Mental Health

Chapter Abstract

The goal of counseling is to produce normalcy in an individual. Various definitions, including Christian ones, of normal and ideal mental health are considered.

Goals for Human Mental Health

Another factor affecting a counseling approach is the set of goals we believe every human being should strive for in terms of mental health. Instead of over-emphasizing categories of abnormality, a qualitatively superior approach to counseling is through the determination of a set of goals appropriate for every human being to strive for in terms of mental health. Psychotherapists may agree on the problems of an emotionally disturbed person, but disagree on the solutions because they have different things they wish to produce in his or her life. It may, at first, seem obvious that the therapy goal for an abnormal personality is to become "normal," but after our discussion of what is normal, we should realize that this approach does not provide clear direction for counseling, especially for those conditions that affect a large number of individuals. We discussed previously that man was "fallen," and that even though 100 percent of men are in this condition at birth and thus fallenness may be   43 normal statistically, it is an unnatural condition for man. Therefore, some other method is needed for defining goals for mental health.

It appears appropriate here to look at some of the attributes of a fully functioning person. Some good suggestions have been made by humanistic psychologists who look to the "ideal" mental health criteria rather than "normal" criteria. Carl Rogers believes that a fully functioning person is one who is open to experience, has an absence of defensiveness, has accurate awareness, unconditional self-regard, and harmonious relationships with others.

Abraham Maslow also has contributed much to our understanding of a fully functioning individual with his theory of self-actualization. He felt that the self-actualizers (persons who make extraordinary use of their potential) like Albert Einstein, Abraham Lincoln, Thomas Jefferson, and Eleanor Roosevelt would be mentally healthy. One criticism of his view, though, is that many of these individuals, such as Lincoln and Roosevelt who are most known for their social concern, did not have very satisfying interpersonal relationships with their spouses and children.

It would be of interest to look at Maslow's characteristics of self-actualizers (adapted from Hilgard, Atkinson, and Atkinson, 1975).[26]

1. They perceive reality efficiently and are able to tolerate uncertainty.

2. They accept themselves and others for what they are.

3. They are spontaneous in thought and behavior.

4. They are problem-centered rather than self-centered.

5. They have a good sense of humor.

6. They are highly creative.

7. They are resistant to enculturation, although not purposively unconventional.

8. They are concerned for the welfare of mankind.

9. They are capable of deep appreciation of the basic experiences of life.

10. They establish deep, satisfying, interpersonal relationships with a few, rather than with many people.

11. They are able to look at life from an objective viewpoint.

These are worthy goals, but they seem so difficult to obtain. The humanist sometimes acts as if man's problem is one of ignorance, that is, he does not know what to do to lead a happy life. Actually, as most of us will attest, a greater problem is our lack of power to do those things we know are right. It is of interest here to compare a Christian psychotherapist's characteristics of mental health with those of Maslow, since a Christian philosophy of man is different in some areas. These are adapted from those of a Christian psychiatrist, O. Quentin Hyder (1971).[27]

1. The mentally healthy person must be in contact with reality and prove this by behaving and reacting to all situations in a realistic way.

2. He should be able to function successfully in the major experiences of life, i.e., vocationally, socially, personally, and sexually.

3. He adapts and adjusts to changed situations with self-control and discipline. He should be free from excessive anxiety or depression in such situations.

4. His actions should not be self-destructive or harmful to others. He must have strong emotional control and accept responsibility for his actions.

5. He will have worthwhile goals in life that he is seeking to achieve within the rules of society. His striving will lead him to some measurement of contentment, happiness, and inner peace.

6. For the Christian, complete health in the whole

man must include a right personal relationship with Jesus Christ as Savior and Lord.

With all of these in mind, we will propose our own goals for human mental health that we believe are most in line with the Bible's teaching on the nature and condition of man and most consistent with the data of psychology.

1. He has begun the integration of his mental and physical being with his spiritual potential by entering into a personal relationship with God through His Son, Jesus Christ.

2. He has purpose in life, including immediate and long-range goals.

3. He has a sense of self-worth that is grounded in at least some unchanging factors.

4. He has the capacity for self-sacrificing love and the empathy and social sensibility this implies.

5. He has an accurate view of reality that remains undistorted by his own needs or pressures arising from his environment.

6. He has strong internal standards so that he can resist undesirable social and environmental pressures.

7. He can react appropriately and with strength and courage in the face of stress and potential or actual suffering. He can accept what is unchangeable.

8. He has a sense of freedom to enjoy himself and is able to derive fun and relaxation out of life.

9. He has the freedom to be creative and a contributor in his work and personal relationships.

10. His physical needs, emotions, and reason are in balance.

It is not likely that all these goals can be accomplished in every counseling case, but by being aware of his overall goals for his counselees, the counselor can set intermediate, specific goals for particular individuals — goals that are in line with what a fully functioning person should be. As we turn our thoughts to application, we will elaborate the outworkings of the foregoing goals.

It is important to state here that Christian psychotherapists do not have hidden agendas or force their specific goals on counselees. One of the first issues to be dealt with in psychotherapy is what the person hopes to get from the counseling process. Thus, the individual begins therapy by defining his goals and the symptoms from which he wants to be relieved. These goals may be expanded or changed later, partly because of the therapist's influence or because new things come to light in treating his problem.

Application of
the Christian View
of Mental Health

Chapter Abstract

With a three-dimensional view of man, Christian counseling can probe all possible sources of problems and integrate scientific and biblical methods to correct them. A person's relationship with God is considered as a major factor in overcoming various problems.

Application of the Christian View of Mental Health

While there is a difference in methods used by Christian psychotherapists, it is possible to discuss some of the basics that should generally distinguish Christian counseling from other models or approaches to counseling. These distinctions stem from a Christian view of man's nature, his problems, and the goals of mental health. The following sections show how Christian counseling is very well suited to deal with all of man's needs and how it can produce the desired factors that contribute to mental health.

Psychotherapy seeks to understand the break-ups in individual personalities and in some way make them whole again. However, to attempt to make man whole again without a blueprint of the whole man and his needs is like driving in a strange city without a map: you soon get lost. Christian psychotherapy has access to God's overall view of man and has the opportunity

The Whole Nature of Man Is Counseled

51

to apply that to the counseling situation. The Christian psychotherapist has a regard for the divine revelation in the Bible and the spiritual power of God in the counseling process. This may appear a naive indulgence to some. However, we believe the inquisitive mind will find sufficient evidence to support a similar confidence. Therefore, the Christian psychotherapist can and wants to minister, not only to man's body and mind, but also to his spiritual needs.

The Christian psychotherapist — who may be a psychiatrist, psychiatric social worker, clinical psychologist, pastor, or other counselor — seeks to combine his personal Christian faith with tried and true counseling techniques. This is stated clearly by Hyder:

> In attempting myself to combine these approaches, using both the results of good professional training and my personal Christian experience and scriptural knowledge, I am hoping to deal more fully with the problems in my patients' lives.[28]

A Christian psychotherapist can *within limits* practice any one of many counseling techniques and approaches; and may choose, like so many counselors today, to use several methods, depending on his skills and the particular problems of his clientele. One should not expect every Christian counselor to use the same method. Some therapists work with a restricted type of client, for whom some techniques may be more effective than others. Behavior modification has been shown to be very effective in dealing with phobias and in modifying some undesirable behavior of hospitalized patients. A therapist working with female divorcees may choose to use a group-therapy approach, whereas a counselor of children may choose not to do so. What is important is that the counselor's Christian beliefs affect the counseling process.

Specifically, counseling the whole man will provide two essential elements to the counseling process. First, the spiritual welfare of the person becomes important to the therapist, since that can affect mental health. It may be that a deficiency in the person's spiritual dimension can be identified and the person helped in this area. Neither are religious individuals immune to emotional problems, marriage difficulties, and other plights, and they often seek professional help. The Christian psychotherapist has a great advantage over his secular counterpart in these situations because he better understands and is more sympathetic to the problems the client faces in living the Christian life. He can propose solutions varying with the spiritual need and understanding of the client. The Christian counselor also has an advantage in that he is in the best position to identify neurotic elements that involve a person's Christian beliefs and to separate these from valid, healthy elements of Christianity. The secular counselor often tries to "relieve" a client from all religion if he suffers from a religiously oriented problem.

Second, God is a part of the counseling process in that He has outlined in the Bible a way for individuals to bring their needs to Him. What God's part involves is summarized by Keith Edwards, associate professor of psychology at Rosemead Graduate School of Psychology:

> In general I believe the major influence of God is through the cognition of both the client and the therapist. As previously noted, Scripture is one of the key sources of such divine influence. Through scriptural truth the client and counselor develop a specific understanding of the problem. Through biblical revelation of the person and work of Christ, the client comes to understand and is motivated by God's love (Romans 2:4). Using scriptural truth as guide, the client and counselor by faith invoke God's appointed means of grace. The latter may include a variety of actions such as prayer, Bible study, fellowship, confession, forgiveness, encouragement, confrontation, etc. These may appear to be rather naturalistic explanations of how "God works" but they are a part of His will and not to be minimized.
>
> I would go a step further and postulate that most of God's supernatural influence on His people is through cognition inspired by the Holy Spirit. It is in the thought life that the spiritual, psychological, and physical interface.[29]

The Christian counselor believes that the ultimate origins of most human difficulties can be traced to

Regeneration of Man's Nature

man's separation from God and all the detrimental effects that that separation has had on man and his world. Although entering into a personal relationship with God through Jesus Christ (and thus "becoming" a Christian) does not solve all of man's problems, it does provide the individual with access to an acceptable (and we believe truthful) world view. Spiritual regeneration also introduces God as an active, present agent in the remaking of the personality through His provision of love, forgiveness, guidance, courage to change, and deepened love relationships with other Christians.

It is important to understand what is meant by a person's being regenerated by God. What is this Christianity that one may embrace? Look at this psychiatrist's definition as explained in *The Kink and I* (Mallory, 1973):

> I have said Christianity is not a neurotic mechanism. It is then, a realistic, healing, elevating system of truth.
>
> I have said Christianity is not just faith in faith. It is, then, a faith in one living and true God as He is made known to us by the Holy Spirit and through Jesus Christ.
>
> I have said Christianity is not just being loving. It is, then, propositional truth which leads us into loving and constructive relationships, and also reveals the true nature of God and all His works.
>
> I have said Christianity is not a happily-ever-after life. It is, then, a continuing struggle, but one in which we can triumph through the power of Christ, and one in which even our defeats, as well as our victories, can contribute to our spiritual and personal growth.
>
> I have said that Christianity is not a poor, second-best psychology. It is, then, the well-spring of relational truth. The best possible source and supply of a well-integrated life.[30]

As can be seen, becoming a Christian is not going to church or giving up enjoyable activities. It is entering into a relationship with God for which man was made. The counselor's interest in this aspect of his client's nature is not for some proselytizing purpose. On the contrary, this new relationship with God opens many life-changing possibilities. In his book, *Emotional Problems and the Gospel,* Vernon Grounds, a leading authority in psychology and theology, discusses the effect of spiritual regeneration on mental health.

> What is essential if mental illness is to be prevented and mental health promoted? For one thing, mental health and healing demand a conviction of life's meaningfulness. . . . But what philosophy meets this demand as adequately as does the biblical faith? If meaningfulness is the antidote for neurosis-creating irrationality, Christianity, I submit, is a powerful ally of mental health. . . .
>
> For a second thing, mental health and healing demand a source of courage which will enable a person to encounter the inescapable anxiety of life. . . . But where is the source of this anxiety-subduing courage to be discovered, a courage which will help an existing individual rise above the threats of futility, guiltiness, and nonbeing? . . . I for one can discover that source nowhere but in the traditional Gospel of Jesus Christ which guarantees a death-annulling resurrection.
>
> For a third thing, mental health and healing demand, on the one hand, the assurance of love, and on the other hand, the power to love. . . . Unless this is in his existence an individual may fall victim to a self-debilitating, neighbor-destroying hate that can end in neurosis. . . . Once more, I fail to see any solution for this problem apart from Christianity. What is the gospel, after all, if not the good news that man . . . a pinpoint of protoplasm on a pigmy planet in a measureless universe, is nevertheless the object of a cosmic love, which gives him ultimate security and ultimate status? . . . What is the gospel, after all, if not the good news that man, curved in egocentricity upon himself, secretly and openly hating his neighbor, can become the subject of outgoing love as the Holy Spirit works within his heart?[31]

The importance of a human being's relationship to God does not mean that a Christian psychotherapist's first order of business is to take advantage of a client's weakened condition and to baptize him on the spot. No, the therapist's first responsibility is to address himself to the immediate needs of the client, who often has calamities in his life that need urgent attention. When confronted with a client who is in need of a change of schedule, job, environment, diet, friendships, or any of a dozen other circumstances, it would be thoughtless and irresponsible of the psychotherapist to counsel him to simply trust God. Usually, when helping with these personal problems, the therapist can trace the immediate distress back to deeper dissatisfactions, such as hatred, loneliness, fear, guilt, or poor self-image. Often, while dealing with these areas, the Christian counselor, perhaps from his own experience, can touch upon the client's need to deal with his spiritual alienation from God, if the client expects any long-term healing of self. If the client sees no need or disagrees, this is no reason for the therapist to refuse further treatment. Not everyone is ready, mentally or emotionally, to make a personal commitment to God. There are still many ways the therapist can help one who is not ready to make such a commitment. In time, the client often begins to see the love and care of God through the therapist's loving, caring attitude, and, as a result, may wish to relate directly to God.

Restructuring of Man's Mind

To repair a disturbed mind, many radical techniques are being used. In est (Erhard Seminars Training), individuals are shouted at, subjected to long, boring lectures, and forbidden to eat or to go to the toilet![32] Another example is brain control by implanted brain electrodes, now being used experimentally to control the destructive urges of man (Delgado, 1971).[33] But these techniques seem to be more destructive of what is human than restorative. These also seem desirable for only the most severe cases of mental disorder, certainly not for the person with a marriage problem or troublesome anxieties and fears. A constructive way of restructuring the mind of man is provided through Christian counseling.

In Christian counseling guilt is met with the recognition of a cleansing, healing forgiveness from God. The client can face problems, since the certainty of forgiveness paves the way to confess, repent, and find healing that comes from setting things right with God and neighbor. An individual's self-image is restructured, not solely along the lines of changeable personal attributes, but by the knowledge of his own creation in the image of God for a purpose. Self-control is developed through prayer and practice. These can help control harmful thoughts and actions that have become habitual. Anger is met with admonition, reason, and the power to love. Lastly, the Christian counselor can give reason and comfort in the face of suffering. A loving, all-powerful God can bring about the best for us, even from our suffering. Let us look at these areas in more detail to see how Christian counseling can deal with these problems as it gives new order to the mind.

Guilt. A Christian psychotherapist can help a person distinguish between three types of guilt: theological, legal, and psychological. Theological guilt comes from a man's separation from God and violation of God's moral law. Legal guilt follows the actual viola-

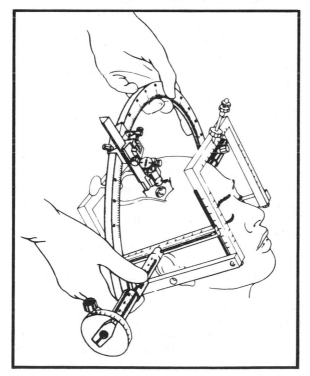

A stereotoxic instrument attached to the head to implant an electrode deep within the brain.

tion of an important social or civil regulation. These two, theological and legal, are the *facts* of guilt and not necessarily the *feelings* of guilt. Psychological guilt is an emotional feeling, generally associated with theological and legal guilt, although it may exist in the absence of any real wrongdoing. Individuals suffering from guilt feelings need to look for and resolve theological and legal guilt in their lives. The solution to theological guilt is not psychotherapy, but setting things right with God through belief in Jesus Christ and what He did to pay the penalty for our sins. True forgiveness is available from God whose moral law we have violated. However, in some cases a sense of forgiveness comes only when trust in God's forgiveness is followed by a sincere effort to make amends to a wronged party. Guilt also can involve self-image problems. While hostility says, "I blame you!" guilt says, "I blame me." Many times the person is not guilty, but only feeling inferior and unworthy.

Self-image. Many of the emotional problems a person faces either come from or lead to an inadequate self-image. Every man, woman, and child has a powerful need to be valuable and worthwhile; but, as we have seen, the world view under which most individuals live has no special basis for assigning a high value to man. If man is just the product of an impersonal universe, from where does his value come? The humanistic psychologist, who has accepted the presuppositions of modern naturalism (i.e., that natural causes explain everything about man), has no basis other than a strong "gut feeling" to argue with B. F. Skinner and the behaviorists in favor of the intrinsic worth of man.

In contrast, the Christian world view says that man *is* valuable because God has declared him so. At first glance, this may seem to be a shallow reason, because modern man tends to look for intrinsic worth in himself. However, how do we arrive at the value of anything we sell in our stores? What someone is willing to pay for an item sets its value. What is man's value? We must ask if anybody wants him and how badly. It so happens that the richest person in the universe, God Himself, loved man so much that He gave the high price of the life of His Son, Jesus Christ, to pay for the consequences of man's sin. That is a source of immense value!

*Emotional problems
are often related to a
person's self-image.*

James Dobson, in his book on self-image in the child, *Hide or Seek,* suggests two powerful artificial systems of value in our society, beauty and intelligence.[34] Some others are: money, business, success, special group membership. Woe be to you if you don't have one or more of these standards of self-image, for you will not be accepted or loved. And yet, even if you have them, you have problems because they are changeable. We grow old and lose our looks and athletic prowess; we have a crippling disease and we lose our money and our job; and so on. There is nothing wrong with good looks, or money, or success; but we need to realize that they will not maintain our self-image. We need to be accepted for just ourselves, no matter what our condition.

At this point we are once again confronted with the relevance of Christianity to mental health. As we said, the person who has problems with his self-image and feels of little worth anticipates rejection, tries to impress, becomes hostile, or behaves in other distinctive ways. But the person who has really and truly found Jesus Christ can answer this identity question in a positive manner. "I am a joint heir with Jesus Christ. I am a son of God. I am tremendously important in the sight of God. Christ died for me, and I am acceptable to Him. He is living within me. We have a union, a relationship. There are also values, principles, ethics, that I can count on. I can follow them. They work."[35]

Breaking habits. Many clients are hopelessly bound by some habitual, debilitating pattern of behavior. Even emotions, through association with various stimulus situations, can become habitual and uncontrollable in similar situations. A person with a genuine Christian commitment has an increased motivation to work on such habits. This motivation results from (1) the promptings of God in his life to progress toward a truly exemplary life of Christian principles, and (2) his own renewed hope in possessing the power from God for change.

A Christian counseling setting can help a person battle with habits by encouraging him to build an ongoing mental process in which he turns constantly to God regarding his weak and vulnerable areas. This has been called *process prayer*.[36] Such interaction between God and a person is not merely the power of positive thinking, a faith with no object, but a belief in a God who is there, who is independent of one's wavering faith, and who will help. In the face of emotional weakness, this process prayer involves continually reflecting on a new relationship with God, thanking God for His love toward the person, asking for specific help to counter the individual's own desires in problem areas, and acting and thinking in ways counter to the individual's destructive habits. The more the person's mind is turned toward God concerning the problem, the more he is consciously in a position to regain control over his unconscious habits.

Anger. Anger is a feeling of tension and aggressiveness that arises within us in frustrating or threatening circumstances. In itself it is not bad, but selfish anger can lead to hostility toward self or others. The importance of anger in emotional problems was stated by Albert Rothenberg, associate professor of psychiatry at Yale University School of Medicine. He said:

> As clinicians, we devote a considerable portion of our thinking and practice to unearthing, clarifying, and tracing the permutations of anger in our patients. In depression we look for evidence of anger behind the saddened aspect; in hysteria we experience angry seductiveness; in homosexuality and sexual disorders, we see angry dependency; in marital problems, we unearth distorted patterns of communication particularly with respect to anger.[37]

One of the first steps in dealing with anger is to recognize anger in ourselves, to honestly plumb the depths of our being and realize how intense our feelings are. This prevents repressing anger or calling it something else. A human being with buried, intense anger is like a volcano, hot and unstable inside and ready to erupt. His anger may explode in the form of his violent temper or bubble over in distressing symptoms such as anxiety, depression, headaches, high blood pressure, and ulcers.

The biblical approach to anger is to avoid reacting out of selfish hostility toward the source of one's anger, and instead to confront that person and attempt to work out the problem. This confrontation, though, must be without condemnation. Hurt feelings should be revealed to the offending party and forgiveness and reconciliation should be pursued. Mental problems do not arise in a vacuum, but in the context of shattered interpersonal relationships. Selfish anger sees one relationship after another shatter. Hatreds build up and unhappiness sets in. Dealing with anger constructively sees communication lines strengthened and love grow. As a result, genuine emotional relief sets in.

Suffering. Human suffering needs to be placed in its proper perspective, so that an individual can accept those things in life that he cannot change. Christianity, which emphasizes life's meaningfulness beyond the physical and psychological comforts of this world, provides such a perspective. While a therapist needs to make every effort to change a client's suffering condition, the client does need to see the benefits that can be derived from suffering. Physical and emotional suffering builds character qualities such as patience, true joy and peace, and empathy for others who suffer. Research on animals and humans shows that subjects exposed to stressful situations are much better able to handle stress in the future.[38] While one should not wish suffering on himself or others, suffering does provide a great opportunity to develop strong personality characteristics that can build mental health and make life worth living. (For the person who cannot accept the seeming contradiction of evil and suffering in the presence of an all-powerful, all-loving God, helpful insight can be had from *The Problem of Pain,* by C. S. Lewis, and *The Roots of Evil* by Norman Geisler, among others.)[39]

**Responsibility
and Reform**

Christian counseling must sometimes guide, direct, and be concerned with the moral behavior of counselees. The counselor's guide for behavior is the Bible, which is a primary source of God's truth for man. God, the architect of man's being, has outlined a pattern of living, which, if followed, is a great source of fulfillment for man. Justification for using the Bible as such a guide rests on the assertion that God exists and has spoken to man and that there is some validation for the authority of the biblical documents and a guarantee that they have survived history intact. This is the impetus behind conservative Christian scholars, who have gathered an impressive amount of evidence for fulfilled biblical prophecies, miracles, the resurrection of Christ, and the survival of the original biblical text (McDowell, 1972; Pinnock, 1971; Ramm, 1953; Wilson, 1977).[40]

It must be realized that psychotherapy is not an amoral enterprise, even for the nondirective counselor, who tries to maintain a value-free atmosphere in the counseling office. No counseling process can be truly value-free and amoral if any communication is going on at all. The only question is whether the therapist is going to be implicit or explicit with his own values.

The question we wish to deal with here concerns the responsibility of the counselee for his condition and the related question of his responsibility to improve. Some schools of psychology — notably those related to the

The counselee's role in arriving at his condition may imply some measure of responsibility for his own improvement.

medical, behavioristic, and the psychoanalytic models — are inclined to shift the responsibility of the emotional disturbance away from the client. The guilty factors are such things as the nervous system, the environment, or early childhood trauma. At least one school of thought believes an individual's mental illness results from his choice of actions, yet this school also believes that faultfinding is wrong as a part of the counseling process. Albert Ellis, who developed rational-emotive therapy, leveled his charge in an article entitled, "There Is No Place for the Concept of Sin in Psychotherapy."[41]

There are, however, growing voices arguing for a rethinking of the responsibility of the patient and even the whole concept of mental "illness" itself. Thomas Szasz, in *The Myth of Mental Illness,* suggests that most mental disorders involve problems in living, problems that ultimately have to be solved by the person who has them.[42]

MEDICAL MODEL

RESPONSIBILITY MODEL

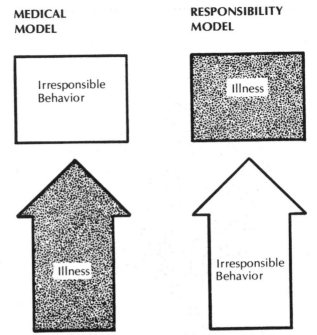

The responsibility model in reverse of the medical model suggests that irresponsible behavior may be a major cause of many mental problems.

Models of responsibility counseling also have been put forward by William Glasser[43] and O. Hobart Mowrer,[44] and by a Christian pastoral counselor, Jay Adams.[45] Mowrer wants to replace the medical model with a moral model. He considers emotionally ill persons guilty persons. Glasser, who developed Reality Therapy, feels that people do not act irresponsibly because they are ill; they are "ill" because they act irresponsibly. He defined responsible behavior as that which meets the person's needs and does so in a way that does not deprive others of the ability to fulfill their needs. The psychology of Mowrer and Glasser is not a religious condemnation of sinful behavior, but a denial of determinism in the mental health picture. Jay Adams, on the other hand, is concerned with the biblical concept of sin, and the effects of sin and guilt on the minds of individuals. "Sin, then, in all of its dimensions, clearly is the problem with which the Christian counselor must grapple" (Adams, 1971).[46]

This issue is far too complicated to resolve to everyone's satisfaction in such a short space, but let us not oversimplify the causes of mental disturbance. As we look at the whole range of mental problems, we must admit that there are many individuals whose bizarre behavior is due primarily to organic accident or strongly ingrained habit patterns. A decision to try harder will not bring these individuals success. However, in defense of responsibility counseling, many problems in adjustment do begin with willful flights from a responsible way of facing life. In time such a life degenerates, and flight from reality becomes easier. Soon a person can be trapped by a cage of his own construction. So both points of view are true. The person slowly puts himself into emotional difficulty; but now he may be trapped and needs help. What help does he need? For most neurotic behavior, at least part of the counseling process should help him begin to act in responsible, moral ways in order to unmake his neurosis and to construct a new life.

By no means would such a counseling approach involve the counselor scolding the counselee about his gross immorality. In spite of criticism to the contrary, directive, biblical counseling can take place without heaping psychological guilt upon a person. The counselor can separate discussions of theological and psychological guilt and can help an individual see his faults without feeling excessive guilt. The advantage of considering counselee responsibility in the counseling process is that the counselee who has a hand in the process has a hope of change. Life is no longer thwarted by a fatalistic, early childhood or by a bad environment. Instead, the counselee can learn to control his actions and feelings, to know in what direction to move, and to proceed with a measure of objectivity and hope.

The Church: The Environment of Care

Many of the poor, the uneducated, the addicted, the criminal, and the mildly disturbed may never seek out professional counseling or have that opportunity, yet they need psychological help. The last ten years has seen the rapid growth of community mental health services to help individuals in their home communities. Such services offer the advantages of immediate care geared for the individual, a shorter treatment time, and no stigma of being sent away to an ''institution.'' The basic emphasis of community health practices is that if assistance in psychological health is needed by large numbers of people, then the counseling apparatus should go to them and seek them out, with preventive as well as therapeutic mental health services. Such services can include consultation and medical health education; brief psychotherapy and crisis intervention; the use of paraprofessionals and nonprofessionals in the counseling process; programs to meet community problems, such as violence, crime, prejudice, unemployment, poverty, political change, unwed mothers, and battered children.

Therapeutic communities also have seen fruitful results in dealing with the emotionally disturbed. Fairweather et al. (1969)[47] demonstrated in a pilot program that newly released mental patients living together as a group (regulating their own behavior, preparing their own meals, even running a handyman business) were better able to achieve meaningful lives in the community than were comparable patients not exposed to the therapeutic community. Responsibility, acceptance, and friendship were very effective in helping these individuals, even those with severe emotional problems.

We would like to suggest that another aspect of Christian counseling can be the use of the local church as a community of individuals meeting each other's deepest needs. People have a need to be loved with self-sacrificing love, with the solicitous empathy and social sensibility this implies. The Christian church should be and can be a place where such love and acceptance abound, a place to be counseled and corrected in loving concern, and a place for the generation gap to be removed. It should be and can be a place where race is no division; where beauty and riches are of no concern; where the poor can go for help; where the unwed mother can be accepted and thus not have to face abortion or rejection; a place where no one is lonely for long; and where, when one hurts, all hurt.

Needless to say, this is not always the picture of the church that Jesus Christ founded. Since men are fallen, the church can become an organization exhibiting legalism, greed, condemnation, and bigotry, to one degree or another, just like any other human institution. We should not reject the institution because at times it has not functioned properly.

Small groups meeting together within a large church can overcome the impersonal dimension, providing vital relationships for needy people.

The church has the potential to heal substantially the men and women and children of our communities. Many Christian counselors use local churches as communities into which they can place some clients, Christian or non-Christian. And from the church they draw individuals to help on a nonprofessional basis in the community mental-health plan. Christian therapists have also helped local churches begin counseling programs within their church communities.

Christian counselors also are helping churches recognize more fully the concept of the body of Christ ministering to its members. The Bible portrays the body of Christ as the whole body of committed Christian believers over the world. Its uniqueness lies in the fact that while Christ is not present physically on earth,

He does indwell each believer spiritually, and thus all believers working together become His body. Effectual believers do what Christ did while He was on earth: love, care, heal, feed, etc. When God reaches out and puts His arms around a suffering person today, He often does it through the arms of His church. One reason this concept is not always a reality in churches is that many have become large, impersonal organizations instead of a collection of needy people, seeking and giving help together. Only in smaller gatherings of Christians meeting together within the church to discuss their needs will this concept take root. From there the concept can reach out to be a vital force in social and mental programs everywhere in the community.

The Effectiveness of Christian Psychotherapy

Chapter Abstract

The results of the various psychotherapies are difficult to determine. The potential effectiveness of Christian psychotherapy, however, is considered superior, because of an emphasis on root problems in all three dimensions of man and on remedies that involve lifelong, life-changing processes.

The Effectiveness of Christian Psychotherapy

It is difficult to measure the effectiveness of Christian psychotherapy, or any psychotherapy for that matter. This is because treatment outcome is influenced by variables pertaining not only to the method but also to the client and the therapist. In addition, it is difficult for psychotherapists to agree on criteria for evaluating client improvement. Is a person better because he thinks he is, or when the therapist feels he has improved? Has the person improved when his behavior is more ''normal,'' or when there has been a resolution of psychic conflict?

Many studies that have evaluated traditional psychotherapy suggest that it is not a panacea to answer all of our mental ills. While some patients dramatically improve in all types of therapy, a small percentage actually get worse, and a large percentage improve at a rate no better than spontaneous improvement could

The Limits of Psychotherapy

produce. Hans Eysenck, in summarizing nineteen studies involving seven thousand cases of psychoanalytic and nonpsychoanalytic types of treatment (behavior modification was not prevalent at that time), found that individuals who received only custodial or general practitioner (M.D.) care improved as much as, or more than, those who received psychotherapy.[48] Eysenck's criterion of improvement was successful social and work adjustment. However, such studies are difficult to control and to interpret. Therefore, more research with better controls and careful measurement is needed. More recent studies report that psychotherapy is effective,[49] or that it works, but that it has limitations.[50]

Assertions of success in psychotherapy are also overinflated by the *hello-goodby* effect and the placebo effect. When a person says "hello" at the beginning of therapy he is more likely to consider himself sick and act accordingly; but by the time he says "goodby" to the counselor, he is more likely to rate himself as improved, in order to rationalize to himself that his time and money have been spent wisely, and to express appreciation to the therapist. The placebo effect

inflates therapy success reports because individuals who think they are receiving effective treatment (even if only a sugar pill) will tend to improve.

The Christian psychotherapist considers the limitations of psychotherapy and believes that a Christian emphasis on the spiritual needs of man, integrated with selected, traditional psychotherapies, provides what is needed for a truly effective psychotherapy. Such an emphasis is in a strong and, we believe, superior position to deal effectively with emotional problems.

Why Do Christians Still Suffer Emotional Problems?

Many ask why it is that Christianity has not produced in its followers the serenity and peace of perfect mental health. Society has not become perfect in the time since Christ, and Christians certainly exhibit their share of mental problems. Christianity has even been accused by such notables as Sigmund Freud and Karl Marx of being a major cause of neurosis, and just a crutch, not a lasting cure, for the emotionally unstable.

In considering these questions, we must first realize that Christianity has often been misinterpreted or misapplied, and thus has not been entirely successful in helping the emotionally disturbed. Some Christians present Christianity as a repressive, guilt-provoking system, instead of a new life of joy, love, and strength in the inner self. Christianity has also been misapplied, in that not everyone who professes to be a Christian has actually embraced a personal relationship with Christ. To such individuals Christianity is only *institutionalized* and not *internalized*. Thus, some of the expected changes in their lives never come about. We should not reject Christianity because it has been improperly interpreted and applied any more than we would reject science because someone invented the atom bomb. We should attempt, instead, to apply it correctly, as Vernon Grounds says:

> In any event, because the gospel is misinterpreted and misapplied we had better exercise care before we make sweeping claims on behalf of its psychic effectiveness. As Christians concerned about the problem of mental illness, we had better set ourselves to the task of serious research

74   and sustained dialogue, attempting to discover why the extraordinary resources of our truths remain untapped.[51]

A second idea that is useful in understanding the effectiveness of Christian psychotherapy is that Christian change represents a lifelong, life-changing process. Christianity speaks of a style of life that is more conducive to optimum physical, mental, social, and spiritual health than any other. The process of gaining health in all these areas cannot be accomplished overnight.

> We are saved for eternity when we believe that Jesus Christ is who He said He was and we trust Him as Lord and Savior. But salvation is also a process of being saved from the chains of egocentricity.
> We are never fully and finally free in this life. But there are relative degrees of freedom in the process of healing. And the person who knows he is loved, who brings what is inside into the light, who takes personal responsibility for his problems, who believes change is possible through Christ, who prays honestly, who forgives and seeks forgiveness, and who practices discipline of mind and process prayer will make great strides toward untwisting his life. . . . (Mallory, 1973)[52]

Because it is a life-changing process, Christian psychotherapy is concerned with root problems and not merely with providing immediate relief from a particular set of symptoms. Therefore, Christian psychotherapy should be evaluated over the lifetime of an individual who has been put on the road to recovery.

At the Atlanta Counseling Center and other Christian counseling centers, the benefit of adding the spiritual dimension to the counseling process has been seen. Therapists utilize many different approaches and techniques based on their own training and personality. However, all believe that a loving God has created every individual with purpose and meaning and that healing and hope are available at the highest level when a person recognizes God's loving, healing power through Jesus Christ and begins to live out the Christian faith.

The goals of psychotherapy to bring symptomatic relief and to help a person grow toward improved mental health are more likely to be realized in a person who can appropriate and apply this faith. Such a person can courageously face all destructive feelings, attitudes, and behavior because he knows that he will not be condemned and that healing and forgiveness are available through Christ. He has an increased motivation and capacity to correct problems and live constructively. If he has previously had neurotic elements in his faith (such as belittlement of self, the provoking of guilt, or "holier-than-thou" attitudes), they are more likely to be alleviated by a Christian counselor who can help recognize these destructive elements without attacking the basic faith. Christian psychotherapy, then, is not a substitute for other well-documented, helpful approaches. Rather, it embraces these in the context of a much-needed additional dimension.

Summary

In summary, this monograph has described a general approach to man and his emotional problems, an approach that we believe is derived from a careful study of the Bible and relevant scientific data. We have sought to show that Christian counseling is admirably suited to deal with man's problems, since it is able to combine proven methods of psychotherapy with a recognition of man's spiritual nature and needs. Christian counseling is particularly appropriate for our emotional problems because it recognizes and treats our whole nature, acknowledging that man's spiritual needs and condition affect his mental life.

To counseling, Christianity offers a remedy for the roots of emotional breakdown, meaning in a meaningless world, reason and comfort in a suffering world, motivation in the face of twisted desire and habit, hope in times of despair and grief, forgiveness where there is guilt, an unchanging and durable basis for self-image, confident direction in living, and a loving community to offer care for those prone to emotional disturbance.

If Christian counseling has not been recognized for its benefits, it is because it has not been applied pervasively in the psychotherapeutic situation. We are confident that this is changing as the antispiritual bias of modern psychology relaxes, as Christian counseling training centers grow, and as Christian psychotherapy proves its relevance in the lives of millions who desperately need emotional help.

Response

Drs. Mallory and Cosgrove rightly emphasize the need to approach mental health with concern for the whole person. The psychotherapist can help not only in the physical and psychological dimensions, but also in the spiritual dimension. It is true that state mental hospital in-patient statistics have been dropping steadily since the introduction of major tranquilizers in the early 1950s. Nevertheless, the loss of man-hours (and woman-hours) from work because of neurotic problems and poor interpersonal relationships is on the increase. More people are seeking private psychiatric help and more are in need of the low-cost or free out-patient psychotherapy clinics being established all over the country by local and state governments, many of which are assisted by federal funding.

O. QUINTEN HYDER

How are the patients being helped? Certainly the use of tranquilizers and antidepressant medications offer symptomatic relief and enable most patients to function and feel better than if they were without them. But the introduction of chemicals into the body can only be of temporary help. This rightly leaves the burden of responsibility on counseling therapy to give attention to the roots of a person's problems, once the symptoms have been reasonably alleviated. However, as Mallory and Cosgrove point out, therapies that deal only with physical and/or psychological dimensions of man are seriously limited in their capacity to remedy human ills. The limited success of treatments based on these two elements of man's nature gives only modest hope of success for present and future treatments based on the same view.

Noting the differing views of man, Mallory and Cosgrove cite evidence in man's very nature for the spiritual dimension: he seems to have an innate awareness of a Being higher than himself, he carries within himself higher moral standards than he can attain, and he is not ultimately satisfied by all the physical and psychological experiences the world can provide.

With this broader view of man for a base of reference, how does a Christian psychotherapist relate to a clientele that includes other religious or philosophical views? Professional ethics dictate that if a person comes to see me desiring a physician-patient relationship, which he understands to be limited to treatment of the physical and psychological, my obligation to him is to respect his expectations. However, during the therapeutic process, I am at liberty to point out to him, if I consider it to be a relevant factor in his constellation of overlapping and interrelating problems, that there is a spiritual dimension he is overlooking. Almost always the missing dimension is indeed a relevant factor, and very rarely has anyone refused to consider it with me after I have thoughtfully brought it to his attention. Whether or not the patient considers the spiritual dimension important in his life and desires to take steps in that area, he may still benefit from some discussion of the moral factors involved with his problems and relationships.

Mallory and Cosgrove have written an excellent treatise, laying very solid foundations upon which the principles of Christian psychotherapy can be based. They have addressed the need for real changes in individual's lives: changes that enable them thereafter to have less fear or anxiety, no longer be depressed, have a greater sense of identity and self-esteem, and relate better to the people with whom they live, work, and socialize. They have given hope for the wholeness of persons and the fulfillment of relationships.

References

[1]James C. Coleman, *Abnormal Psychology and Modern Life*, 4th ed. (Glenview, Ill.: Scott F, 1972), p. 10.

[2]Paul Meehl, et al., eds., *What, Then, Is Man? A Symposium of Theology, Psychology, and Psychiatry* (St. Louis: Concordia, 1958); Frank C. Peters, "Counseling and Evangelical Theology," *Bibliotheca Sacra*, 126 (1969): 3-15; Craig W. Ellison, "Christianity and Psychology: Contradictory or Complimentary?" *Journal of the American Scientific Affiliation*, 24 (1972): 131-134; Kirk E. Farnsworth, "Psychology and Christianity: A Substantial Integration," *Journal of the American Scientific Affiliation*, 27 (1975): 60-66; Art Greer, *No Grown-Ups in Heaven. A T-A Primer for Christians (and others)* (New York: Hawthorn Books, with Clement Stone, Publisher, 1975); Basil Jackson, "The Psyche in Psychology and Theology," *Journal of Psychology and Theology*, 3 (1975): 3-10; Millard J. Sall, *Faith, Psychology and Christian Maturity* (Grand Rapids: Zondervan, 1975).

[3]John D. Carter and Richard J. Mohline, "The Nature and Scope of Integration: A Proposal," *Journal of Psychology and Theology*, 4 (1976): 4.

[4]Abraham Maslow, *Motivation and Personality,* 2nd ed. (New York: Harper, 1970).

[5]Desmond Morris, *The Naked Ape* (New York: Dell, 1967).

[6]A discussion of the uniqueness of human nature can be found in another monograph in this series by Mark P. Cosgrove, *The Essence of Human Nature* (Grand Rapids: Zondervan, 1977).

[7]Abraham Maslow, *Toward a Psychology of Being* (Princeton, N.J.: D. Van Nostrand, 1962); Carl Rogers, *On Becoming a Person* (Boston: Houghton Mifflin, 1961).

[8]Harry Stack Sullivan, *The Interpersonal Theory of Psychiatry* (New York: Norton, 1953); Erich Fromm, *The Anatomy of Human Destruction* (New York: Holt, Rinehart and Winston, 1973); Karen Horney, *Neurosis and Human Growth* (New York: Norton, 1950); Eric Berne, *Games People Play* (New York: Grove Press, 1964).

[9]S. I. McMillen, *None of These Diseases* (Old Tappan, N.J.: Revell, 1963).

[10]J. V. Brady, R. W. Porter, D. G. Conrad, and J. W. Mason, "Avoidance Behavior and the Development of Gastroduodenal Ulcers," *Journal of the Experimental Analysis of Behavior*, 1 (1958): 69-73.

[11]Meyer Friedman and Ray Toseman, *Type A Behavior and Your Heart* (New York: Knopf, 1974).

[12]Viktor Frankl, *Man's Search For Meaning* (Boston: Beacon Press, 1959); John J. Shea, "On the Place of Religion in the Thought of Viktor Frankl," *Journal of Psychology and Theology,* 3 (1975): 179-186.

[13]Maslow, *Toward a Psychology of Being,* p. 3.

[14]John B. Watson, "Experimental Studies on the Growth of Emotions," in C. Murchison, ed., *Psychologies of 1925* (Worcester, Mass: Clark University Press, 1926).

[15]Maslow, *Toward a Psychology of Being,* p. 10.

[16]Lawrence Kohlberg, "Development of Moral Character and Moral Ideology," in M. L. Hoffman and L. W. Hoffman, eds., *Review of Child Development Research* (New York: Russell Sage Foundation, 1964).

[17]B. F. Skinner, *Beyond Freedom and Dignity* (New York: Knopf, 1971).

[18]Floyd L. Ruch and Phillip G. Zimbardo, *Psychology and Life,* 8th ed. (Glenview, Ill.: Scott F, 1971), p. 526.

[19]Stanley Milgram, "Behavioral Study of Obedience," *Journal of Abnormal and Social Psychology,* 67 (1963): 361-378.

[20]"Morals Make a Comeback," *Time,* September 15 (1975): p. 94.

[21]*The Diagnostic and Statistical Manual of Mental Disorders,* 2nd ed. (Washington, D.C.: The American Psychiatric Association, 1968).

[22]L. L. Heston, "The Genetics of Schizophrenic Disease," *Science,* 167 (1970): 249-256.

[23]James C. Coleman, *Abnormal Psychology and Modern Life.* 4th ed. (Glenview, Ill.: Scott F, 1972).

[24]James Sire, *The Universe Next Door* (Downers Grove, Ill.: InterVarsity Press, 1976).

[25]Rollo R. May, *The Art of Counseling* (Nashville: Abingdon, 1967), p. 28.

[26]Ernest R. Hilgard, Richard C. Atkinson, and Rita L. Atkinson, *Introduction to Psychology,* 6th ed. (New York: Harcourt, Brace Jovanovich, 1975), p. 393.

[27]O. Quentin Hyder, *The Christian's Handbook of Psychiatry* (Old Tappan, N.J.: Revell, 1971), pp. 50, 51.

[28]Ibid., p. 176.

[29] Keith J. Edwards, "Effective Counseling and Psychotherapy: An Integrative Review of Research," *Journal of Psychology and Theology*, 4 (1976): p. 104.

[30] James D. Mallory, *The Kink and I, A Psychiatrist's Guide to Untwisted Living* (Grand Rapids: Zondervan, 1973), p. 76.

[31] Vernon Grounds, *Emotional Problems and the Gospel* (Grand Rapids: Zondervan, 1976), pp. 101,102.

[32] Nathaniel Lande *Mindstyles/Lifestyles* (Los Angeles: Price, Stern, Sloan, 1976).

[33] Jose M. R. Delgado, *Physical Control of the Mind: Toward a Psychocivilized Society* (New York: Harper, 1971).

[34] James Dobson, *Hide or Seek* (Old Tappan, N.J.: Revell, 1974).

[35] Mallory, *The Kink and I*, pp. 109,110.

[36] Ibid.

[37] Albert Rothenberg, quoted in Vernon Grounds, *Emotional Problems and the Gospel* (Grand Rapids: Zondervan, 1976), pp. 51, 52.

[38] J. L. Hess, V. H. Denenberg, M. X. Zarrow, and W. D. Pfeifer, "Modification of the Plasma Corticosterone Response Curve as a Function of Stimulation in Infancy," *Physiology and Behavior*, 4 (1969): 109-111.

[39] C. S. Lewis, *The Problem of Pain* (London: Geoffrey Bles, 1940; New York: Macmillan, 1962), and Norman L. Geisler; *The Roots of Evil* (Grand Rapids: Zondervan, 1978).

[40] Josh McDowell, *Evidence That Demands a Verdict* (San Bernardino: Campus Crusade for Christ, 1972); Clark Pinnock, *Set Forth Your Case* (Chicago: Moody, 1971); Bernard Ramm, *Protestant Christian Evidences* (Chicago: Moody, 1953); Clifford L. Wilson, *Rocks, Relics and Biblical Reliability* (Grand Rapids: Zondervan, 1977).

[41] Albert Ellis, "There Is No Place for the Concept of Sin in Psychotherapy," *Journal of Counseling Psychology*, 7 (1960): 191,192.

[42] Thomas Szasz, *The Myth of Mental Illness* (New York: Dell, 1960).

[43] William Glasser, *Reality Therapy: A New Approach to Psychiatry* (New York: Harper, 1965).

[44] O. Hobart Mowrer, *The Crisis in Psychiatry and Religion* (Princeton: Van Nostrand Co., 1961).

[45] Jay E. Adams, *Competent to Counsel* (Grand Rapids: Baker, 1971).

[46] Jay E. Adams, *The Christian Counselor's Manual* (Grand Rapids: Baker, 1973), p. 124.

[47] G. W. Fairweather, D. H. Sanders, R. F. Maynard, and D. L. Cressler, *Community Life for the Mentally Ill: Alternative to Institutional Care* (Chicago: Aldine, 1969).

[48] Hans J. Eysenck, "The Effects of Psychotherapy: An Evaluation," *Journal of Consulting Psychology,* 16 (1952): 319-324.

[49] J. Meltzoff and M. Kornreich, "It Works," *Psychology Today,* 5 (1971): 57-61.

[50] L. Lubrosky, M. Chandler, A. H. Auerback, J. Cohen, and H. M. Bacrach, "Factors Influencing the Outcome of Therapy," *Psychological Bulletin,* 75 (1971): 145-185; Allen E. Bergin, "When Shrinks Hurt: Psychotherapy Can Be Dangerous," *Psychology Today,* 9 (1975): 96-100.

[51] Grounds, *Emotional Problems and the Gospel,* p. 109.

[52] Mallory, *The Kink and I,* p. 224.

For Further Reading

Journal of Psychology and Theology. Published by Rosemead Graduate School of Psychology. 13800 Biola Avenue, La Mirada, Calif. 90639.

This is an excellent journal whose purpose is to communicate recent scholarly thinking on the interrelationship of psychological and theological concepts and to consider the application of these concepts to a variety of professional settings.

Collins, Gary. **The Rebuilding of Psychology: An Integration of Psychology and Christianity.** Wheaton, Ill. Tyndale House Publishers, 1977.

One of the most popular authors integrating psychology and Christianity gives an overview and evaluation of Christian contributions to psychology, arguing that to make psychology truly relevant, it must be built on a biblical foundation.

Crabb, Larry. **Effective Biblical Counseling.** Grand Rapids, Mich.: Zondervan Publishing House, 1977.

Crabb writes from the conviction that the local church should and can successfully resume responsibility within its ranks for restoring troubled people to full, productive, creative lives.

Grounds, Vernon. **Emotional Problems and the Gospel.** Grand Rapids, Mich.: Zondervan Publishing House, 1976.

The author, who has a B.D. in theology and a Ph.D. in psychology, makes a practical application of the Christian gospel message to emotional problems.

Jeeves, Malcolm. **Psychology & Christianity: The View Both Ways.** Downers Grove, Ill.: InterVarsity Press, 1976.

This is an excellent book, integrating psychology and Christianity, by a professor of experimental neuropsychology.

Mallory, James. **The Kink and I: A Psychiatrist's Guide to Untwisted Living.** Wheaton, Ill.: Victor Books, 1973.

This is a very practical, well-written book on the interrelationship of psychiatric and biblical counsel applied to everyday problems in living.

Meehl, Paul et al., ed. **What, Then, Is Man? A Symposium of Theology, Psychology, and Psychiatry.** St. Louis, Mo: Concordia Publishing House, 1958.

This is one of the most scholarly sources available for examining the issues on the nature of man and mental health from a Christian perspective.

Hyder, O. Quentin. **The Christian's Handbook of Psychiatry.** Westwood, N. J.: Revell, 1971.

In his book, Dr. Hyder gives clear and readable guidelines for handling organic brain diseases, depression, guilt, anxiety, repression of memory, and psychosomatic disorders. This is not a how-to manual but an easily understood discussion of problems and solutions through the application of a form of responsibility therapy.

Notes